How to draw
MACHINES

Written and Illustrated
by Barry Green
Edited by Simon Mugford

First published in Great Britain by Funfax Ltd.,
an imprint of Dorling Kindersley Limited,
9 Henrietta Street, London WC2E 8PS
Funfax concept © Funfax Ltd.
Text and illustrations © 2000 Funfax Ltd.
© & TM The Media Merchants TV Co Ltd.

TOOLS AND MATERIALS

Paper

If you just want to practise your drawing skills, use cheap paper you won't mind throwing away if you don't like the results. You could use the plain back of scrap paper. If you are drawing a picture you want to keep, cartridge paper is good to use and can be bought in pads of different sizes.

Pencils

Start your drawings using a 2H or HB pencil. A 2H pencil makes hard, faint lines. It is good for planning out your picture, but the lines can be difficult to rub out if you press too hard.

Pens

Once you have your pencil drawing as you'd like it, outline it using a black fineliner pen then rub out all the pencil lines. If you are using felt-tip pens or paints to colour the picture in, it's best to use a waterproof black pen so that you won't smudge your lines.

Keep a small sketchbook and a pencil with you wherever you go, then you can draw interesting things you see. The more you draw, the better you'll become!

COLOURING IN

Coloured pencils
You can colour in your picture using coloured pencils. Start off lightly then gradually darken the colour by pressing harder.

Felt-tip pens
These are good for colouring in, especially when you want nice bright colours.

Poster paints or acrylics
These paints are great for mixing together to create new colours. Tone down their colour by adding more water or by mixing in white.

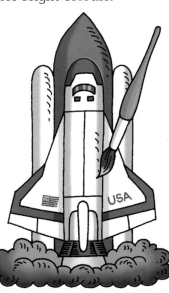

Tip

A good way of colouring in is to use felt-tip pens or paints as a base, then add shading with coloured pencils.

TECHNIQUES

When you are drawing machines, you will find that these are the most common shapes you use:

Square

Circle   **Oval**   **Rectangle**   **Triangles**

Drawing machines often involves using straight lines and angles. Here's a good way of getting these right...

1. On a piece of tracing paper, draw a grid as shown.

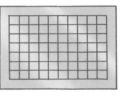

2. Place the tracing paper over a picture that you want to copy.

3. On a normal piece of paper, lightly sketch a grid with the same amount of squares. This grid can be any size. Now copy the picture, square by square. Go over your picture in pen and rub out the pencil lines afterwards.

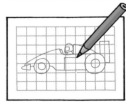

Circles can be difficult to draw freehand. You could draw around a circular object but the best way is to use a compass.

Freehand circles
If you want to try drawing circles freehand, try this method.

1. Draw a square.

2. Draw lines in the square as shown.

3. You can now use the triangular shapes as a guide for your circle.

4. Use the same method to draw ovals. (Draw a rectangle instead of a square.)

To get the effect of a wheel moving at speed, draw an oval shape positioned at a slight angle. Add 'movement lines' to emphasise the effect.

A BASIC CAR

To get you started, here's a simple way to draw a basic car.

1 Using a pencil, lightly draw two rectangles for the car body and two circles for the wheels.

2 Sketch in the shape of the car body.

Add in details such as lights and bumpers. Ink in the lines with a fineliner, and rub out the pencil lines.

Use this technique (pencilling, inking in and rubbing out) to draw all the machines in this book.

3-D CAR VIEW

You can draw a basic car from a different view by following these easy steps.

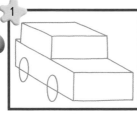

1

Draw two box shapes as shown. Add two ovals for the wheels.

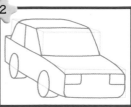

2

Draw in the outline of the car. Add curved lines to the ovals to complete the wheels as shown. You can add details such as headlamps at this stage.

From this view, you can draw in things like the radiator grille and number plate.

Tip

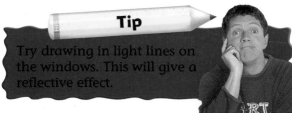

Try drawing in light lines on the windows. This will give a reflective effect.

SPORTS CAR

This sports car has a much curvier look than the cars on the previous pages.

1 Draw a rectangle for the body, and a curved line for the roof. Draw in two ovals at angles for the wheels.

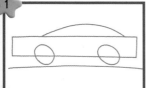

2 Give the car a curved body, and add the sporty details. Details such as alloy wheels and a spoiler will make it look really smart.

Movement lines drawn in behind the wheels will make it look as if it's moving very fast. You could give it a 'two-tone' paint job.

DRAGSTER

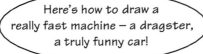

Here's how to draw a really fast machine – a dragster, a truly funny car!

Draw a triangular shape with a blunt end and a curved shape for the cockpit. The two oval-shaped wheels need to be different sizes – the rear one larger than the front.

Draw in the body shape and details as shown. This dragster has a 'wheelie bar' to stop it tipping over when it accelerates.

Finish off by adding a pattern to the dragster, and then put in some movement lines and smoke for effect. Vrrroooommm!

9

JEEP

It's time to get wild and muddy with this great off-roader.

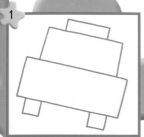

1

2

Draw three rectangles at an angle as shown and add two squares for the wheels.

Now start to add the details. This jeep has a large radiator grille and big wing mirrors.

Finish off your jeep by filling in the detail on the tyres (including the one on the roof). Draw in some mud and movement lines.

F1 RACING CAR

This Formula 1 racing car is one of the
fastest cars around.

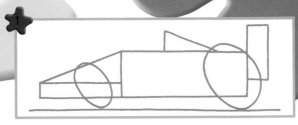

Draw simple outline shapes as shown.
Add in ovals at angles for the wheels.

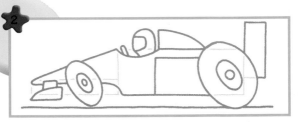

Now draw in the shape of the body. Add in
details such as the driver and steering wheel.

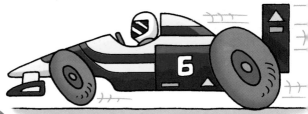

You could use the design shown here, or
copy one from a picture of a real Formula 1
car. Add reflection lines to the driver's visor
and movement lines for speed.

BIGFOOT TRUCK

Car-crushing Bigfoot is a real monster of a truck!

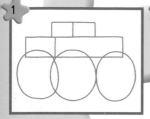

Draw two rectangular boxes for the body and three large oval shapes for the wheels.

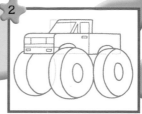

Add the details shown – note the wheel arches. Complete the shape of the wheels and tyres by making them big and fat!

To finish off, add details such as the axle between the front wheels and the big, chunky treads on the tyres.

GIANT DUMP TRUCK

There are lots of triangular shapes to draw on this giant earth-moving truck.

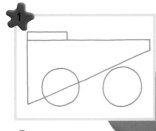

1 Start by drawing a triangular shape with a small rectangle on the top left-hand side. Draw two circles for wheels as shown.

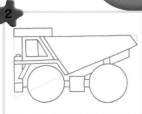

2 Add lines around the wheels for the chassis and start to draw in the detail for the driver's cab.

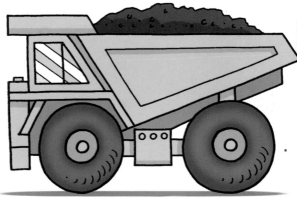

Finish off by drawing in the wheel hubs (the tyres are big) and the truck's chassis. Don't forget to fill the truck with soil.

BULLDOZER

Here's another earth-mover to draw.

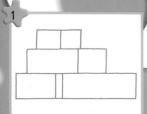

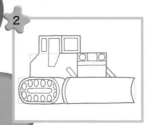

Two boxes on top of a large rectangle form the outline. Add two vertical lines inside the rectangle as shown.

Draw in details. Use the vertical lines in the rectangle as a guide for shaping the caterpillar tracks and the blade.

Finish your bulldozer by adding in the caterpillar tracks and the exhaust pipe shown here. Draw in some earth and some movement lines to make it look as if it's shaking. Now it's ready to go to work!

14

TANK

Use greens and browns to colour in this terrific tank.

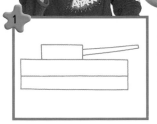

1 Draw three rectangles as shown. The tank's gun is a long, tapered rectangle. (It's slightly wider nearer the turret.)

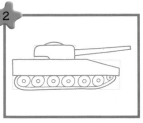

2 Draw in the shape of the turret and the body. Next, draw in the caterpillar tracks as shown.

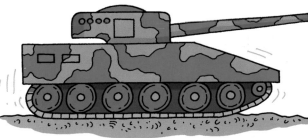

Finish off the tank's detail. Draw in the sections of the caterpillar tracks and any other parts. Give your tank a camouflage pattern and colour in.

Now's your chance to draw a two-wheeled, pedal-powered machine – a bike!

1

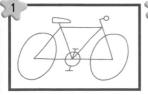

Draw an M-shaped frame as shown. Add oval-shaped wheels and the outlines of the pedals, seat and handlebars.

2

Following the guidelines, 'flesh' out the frame and other details. Don't forget to add the tyres.

3

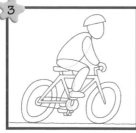

You could add a rider by drawing in the shapes shown here. If you've never drawn people before, just keep the shapes simple and take your time.

4

Finish your picture by adding lines to show speed – don't forget the rider's safety helmet!

CHOPPER BIKE

This chopper motorbike is a real mean machine.

1

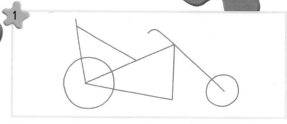

Draw two triangles and two circles for the outline. The handlebars and front fork have a straight line with a slightly curved end.

2

Carefully add in the details. Draw in the fuel tank, lights, the double-seat and the exhaust pipes.

The engine needs a lot of attention to detail. You could use silver pen to colour some of it in. Born to be wild!

MOTORBIKE

Here's how to draw a two-wheeled dream machine!

1

The basic motorbike shape is formed from triangular shapes and circles. Draw a curved outline at the top left for the windshield.

Follow the guidelines to draw in the shape of the frame. Add in the handlebars, the wheels, forks and exhaust pipe.

2

Only a small part of the engine is visible. Colour in the bodywork and add the headlights and some reflective marks.

RACING MOTORBIKE

Here's a racing superbike and rider.

Draw the outline of the bike and rider together. Just follow the shapes as shown here. The wheels are angled ovals to show the bike taking a corner.

Shape the frame and add in the rider's arm and leg. Draw in the front and back wheels, the forks and the exhaust.

Finish off the motorbike with details such as those shown here. The driver's leathers and the bike should be in matching colours.

STEAM TRAIN

Follow the steps to draw this steam locomotive.

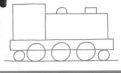

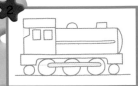

For the outline, draw the rectangular and square shapes shown here. There are five wheels.

Draw in the body shape and add details such as the windows and wheel rod. Give the front a rounded shape.

Finishing details include the buffers and a good plume of steam. Add detail to the wheels and draw in the track underneath. All aboard!

HIGH-SPEED TRAIN

Now you can draw a 200 mph super train!

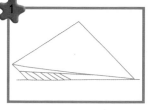

Sketch this triangular shape for the outline of the train speeding in from the distance. The guides for the rail lines are shown at the bottom.

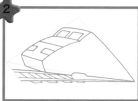

Draw in the train's shape and add in windows and lights. Draw in the visible part of the track.

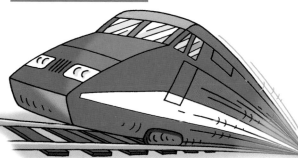

Finish off the details as shown. Add lots of movement lines and colour in.

Tip

Use lighter colours towards the rear of the train – this helps to give an impression of distance.

SAILING SHIP

Set sail to days of old with this square-rigged galleon.

1

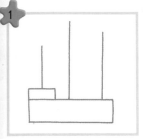

Draw two rectangles and three vertical lines for the basic shape. This is the outline for the hull and masts.

2

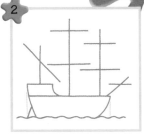

Draw in the galleon's hull and add cross-stays to the masts. Draw in wavy lines for the sea.

Finish off by adding sails and flags to the masts. It's easier to draw the front sails in first and work back. Draw in the wooden detail on the hull and add movement lines to show the sails are fully set.

HOVERCRAFT

Follow the steps to draw this cross-channel hovering machine.

1 Draw the rectangles and boxes shown here. Add narrow ovals for the spinning propeller blades.

2 Draw in the curved shape of the hovercraft's body and skirts. Add details such as windows.

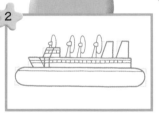

To finish, add a foaming sea. You might like to add some kind of logo to the funnels.

SPEEDBOAT

Here's how to draw a high-speed marine machine.

1

Draw a tapered rectangular shape as shown here. Add a triangle on top and at the front, and draw in a wavy line for the sea.

2

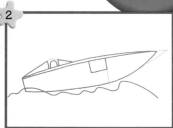

Shape the speedboat's hull as shown and add details. Don't forget the driver.

Finish off by adding lines around the hull to show speed, and complete the waves. The waves shouldn't touch the front because the nose lifts as it powers through the water.

CRUISE SHIP

Follow the steps to draw this luxury liner.

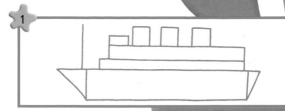

1

Draw the simple rectangular shapes as shown. Add a triangle to the front. A line forms the mast at the bow of the ship.

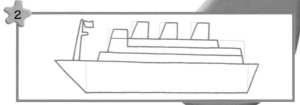

2

Draw in the rest of the ship using the shapes as a guide. Start to add details such as the mast and flag.

Add all the finishing touches – the portholes, lifeboats and logo on the funnel. Don't forget to draw in the sea.

AEROPLANE

This jetliner is just taking off.

1

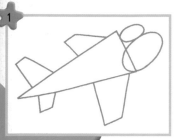

Draw a few simple triangles and a couple of ovals to form the basic outline of the plane.

2

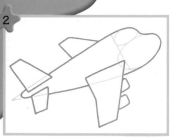

Use the shapes as a guide to sketch the plane's shape. Carefully draw the wings and engines.

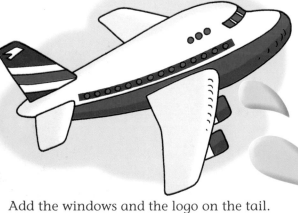

Add the windows and the logo on the tail. Now you're off!

JET FIGHTER

This jet fighter has a super-sleek shape for supersonic speed.

Show the body of the plane with an angled rectangle. Draw a few simple triangles for the wings and fins.

1

Sketch in the cockpit as shown and shape the wings and fins. Note the missile under the wing.

2

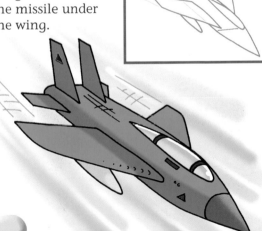

Complete the fighter by adding detail. Draw in the cockpit cover and add movement lines for that speedy, supersonic effect!

LIGHT AIRCRAFT

Follow the steps to draw this light aircraft.

1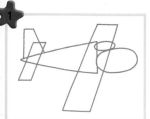

Draw the basic outline shapes shown here to start.

2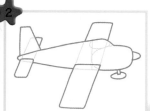

Sketch the shape of the aircraft and start to add details such as the landing gear.

Now you can finish off by adding the windows and the propeller. Draw in the plane's control surfaces (flaps, rudder and so on), add colour and your plane is ready to take to the skies!

HELICOPTER

Try drawing this hovering machine.

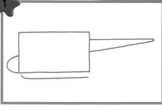

1 The basic outline is a rectangle, a small semi-circle and a long, thin triangular shape.

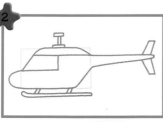

2 Draw in the main body shape and details such as the window and tail. Add the helicopter's landing skid.

Finish off by drawing in the rotor blades and the tail rotor. Colour in and add reflection lines to the windows. Add some movement lines.

SPACE SHUTTLE

Try drawing this reusable spacecraft.

1

Draw these shapes for the guidelines of the Space Shuttle.

2

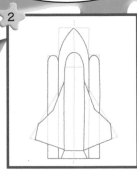

Add shape to the Shuttle's main fuel tanks and booster rockets. Now draw in the wing shape.

3

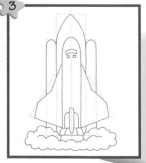

Draw in the cockpit windows, the tail and start to sketch the blast from the rocket.

4

Finish off by adding the minor details. Complete the blast and add a 'NASA' logo if you like.

UFO

Here's a machine that's truly out of this world!

1

2

For the outline, draw these triangular shapes as shown.

Shape the UFO and add in the alien details.

Finish off the details. This is a fantasy spacecraft, so you can use your imagination to create a really wacky design.

ROBOT

Here's a machine man for you to create.

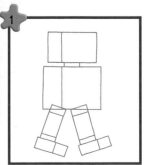

Draw these simple rectangular and square outlines.

Draw in the head, arms and legs, and add further details as shown.

Use your imagination for the finishing touches. Give your metal man a silvery finish for a truly metallic look.